P9-DMW-179

NO. 1 ARTS & CRAFTS OF JAPAN

Masks

Text by

SEIROKU NOMA

English adaptation by

MEREDITH WEATHERBY

CHARLES E. TUTTLE COMPANY

RUTLAND, VERMONT & TOKYO, JAPAN

Publisher's Note

The text which follows, though adapted for Western readers and slightly changed because of space considerations, is based directly upon Professor Noma's excellent Japanese text, as translated by Masaru Muro and Yoshiko Tezuka. The careful reader will note an occasional inconsistency of style or fact between the English captions beside the plates, prepared at the time of the original Japanese edition, and the English text, especially prepared and, where necessary, corrected for this edition. We believe the reader will agree, however, that these slight inconsistencies are more than offset by the quality of the text and plates themselves.

Published by the Charles E. Tuttle Company, of Rutland, Vermont & Tokyo, Japan, by arrangement with Kodansha, Tokyo.

Library of Congress Catalog Card No. 57–8793

First English edition, March, 1957

Printed in Japan by Dai Nippon Printing Co., Tokyo

1 伎楽　太孤父　東大寺蔵　8 世紀
GIGAKU MASK: TAIKOFU.
8th century. *Tōdaiji Temple, Nara.*

Masks

The date of man's invention of masks is not known, but since they are found in wide use in such primitive cultures as those of the Alaskan snowfields, aboriginal Africa, and the islands of the South Seas, their use is certainly several thousands of years old. And, while we have no examples of these earliest masks, we can easily imagine that they must have been very similar in appearance to those still in use by savage tribes. The very fact that masks in one form or another have made their appearance in every culture shows how important a role they have played in human life.

What then was the original purpose of masks? They appeared when man first thought of gods and feared devils. Primitive man, puzzled and awed by the might of nature, attributed nature's manifestations to the gods and took such disasters as storms, floods, and diseases to be the work of devils. Unable to conceive his gods and devils in the abstract, man imagined them to have bodies very similar to his own, yet somehow distinctly different, figures not seen among men. Even today we ourselves often picture gods and devils in our minds, much as did our ancestors. They organized festivals for the purpose of praying to the gods and pacifying the devils. In such festivals it was necessary for humans to act the roles of the gods and devils, and some distinguishing mark was needed for the purpose. It was out of this need that masks evolved.

Thus it was that early masks were not made to resemble human faces but rather to attempt to suggest something supernatural and strange, something that had never been seen among men. Animal-like masks with horns, bird-like masks with bills, strange nightmare carvings with enormous eyes—all these gave the beholder a feeling of the supernatural. In time these same sinister representations were extended to embrace not only divinities but their semi-divine servitors as well and, sometimes, the users' own ancestors. And the earliest rituals, gradually developing into the presentation of legends peculiar and holy to a specific tribe, came in time to be the dance and drama as we know it today among primitive peoples.

With the development of dance and true drama, masks became less primitive and more artistic. Even after the techniques of adorning the face with make-up came into use, masks still served their purpose of creating stronger and more fantastic effects than could ever be achieved with make-up. The very immobility of a mask, which seems such a disadvantage when compared with the living human face, has about it a certain air of the supernatural and fantastic. It is this fact which accounts for the continued use of masks down to the present day.

Among the peoples of the world who still actively use masks, the Japanese are in many ways outstanding. Not only are their masks quite artistic and rich in variety, but they are also still widely used in Japan even today. Although masks undoubtedly first came to Japan from the Asiatic mainland, today they are no longer much used there, and hence it is in Japan that the Asiatic mask has survived and seen its greatest development. This very survival itself is witness to the innate love the Japanese people have for masks.

The formal history of the masks of Japan, as we know them today, opens with the introduction of the dance-drama form called Gigaku from the continent in the sixth century. In the seventh century, again from the mainland, another form of dance-drama, called Bugaku, was introduced and, gradually supplanting Gigaku in popularity, survives today. Then, during the eighth or ninth centuries, there was introduced the practice of using masks in the form of the Buddhist ceremony called Gyodo. This use of the mask by Buddhism, which was then sweeping the country, popularized the mask much more widely than had the more exclusively aristocratic Gigaku and Bugaku. Thus it was in the main under the influence of Gyodo that popular masked plays developed in Japan, the crude masks of the Gyodo ceremony being gradually refined and developed until they became the exquisite masks now used in the familiar dramatic forms of Noh and Kyogen. The Noh and Kyogen masks were still further popularized and developed into the Kagura masks used in every city and hamlet throughout the nation. Thus the development of the mask in Japan has been like the propagation of flowers from seeds, each flower producing the seed for yet other flowers, which in turn yield more seeds and yet more flowers.

Gigaku

The masks used in the Gigaku dance-drama are not only the first historic masks used in Japan but are among the oldest surviving examples of masks in the entire world. Gigaku came to Japan from a kingdom of central China called Go (the kingdom is called Wu in Chinese, Go being the Japanese reading of the same ideograph) and was properly called Gogaku, i.e., "the music of Go," but it soon came to be known by the name still used today, Gigaku, "skillful music," as the music which accompanied the dance was so far advanced over the immature native music of Japan. It is generally believed that a member of the royal family of Go came and settled in Japan in the middle of the sixth century, bringing with him the musical instruments and masks of his native state. However, the first record of actual Gigaku performances in Japan is that of the year 612, when Mimashi, who had learned Gigaku in Go, came to Japan by way of the Korean kingdom of Kudara. This was the period when Japan, under the leadership of the gifted crown prince Shotoku Taishi, was eagerly adopting Chinese culture and Chinese Buddhism; the imperial court welcomed

Mimashi with open arms, appointing two carefully selected youths to learn Gigaku from him in order to pass the art down to their descendants. Under the impetus of this great esteem, Gigaku continued to flourish in Japan, performed both at the imperial court and in the great Buddhist temples, for more than two centuries until it was finally supplanted about the ninth century by Bugaku.

As Gigaku no longer exists today, our only idea of what it must have been like comes from ancient descriptions of its performance. Judging from the principal such source, an ancient document known as the *Kyokunsho,* Gigaku was in the nature of a comic dance performed outdoors, say in a temple courtyard, similar in many ways to the masked dances of Lamaism, but differing from these in that it was less religious and more comical in character. The cast of characters, in order of appearance, each having his own particular mask, were Shishi *(Plate 31),* Shishiko *(Plate 13),* Chido *(Plate 14),* Goko *(Plate 11),* Kongo, Karura *(Plate 7),* Konron *(Plate 15),* Gojo *(Plate 16),* Rikishi *(Plate 10),* Taikofu *(Plate 1),* Taikoji, Baramon *(Plate 12),* Suiko-o *(Plate 18),* and Suikoju *(Plate 17).*

First came Shishi, the lion, led by the two lion-taming boys called Shishiko. Next came a character called Chido and a king called Goko, neither of whom had much part to play but only excited the audience's anticipation with their imposing mien. Then sturdy Kongo came tramping in, followed by the nimbly moving Karura in the shape of a bird. At this point the action became quite fast. Konron appeared, the dreadful appearance of his grotesque mask offset by his laughter-provoking gestures. Contrasting with Konron, then came the delicate and beautiful girl Gojo, to whom the grotesque Konron made a comic pantomime of love. Rikishi, the girl's escort, became angry and there ensued the buffoonery of a fight between Rikishi and Konron, ending with the breaking off of Konron's phallus. There was certainly an element of broad, coarse humor in the attachment of the ugly old man for the beautiful young girl and in this unhappy end of the affair. Before the laughter had ceased, the old man Taikofu came tottering in, supported by the boy named Taikoji. Something in the man's feeble gait again provoked laughter, and then, in contrast, came Baramon (i.e., a Brahman or member of the highest

2 舞楽 蘭陵王 東大寺蔵 12 世紀
BUGAKU MASK: RANRYŌ-Ō.
12th century. *Tōdaiji Temple, Nara.*

Hindu caste), waving a long piece of cloth as though he were an acrobat. After the sluggish motions of old Taikofu, the eyes of the audience danced with delight to see this great activity. And finally came the foreign king, Suiko-o, followed by his eight attendants, called Suikoju; as their names suggest in Japanese, both king and his attendants were all drunkards. Reinforcing the comical impression of their masks with drunken gestures, they brought the audience's laughter to its final climax.

This was the Gigaku performance, and though it can no longer be seen today, echoes of its mirth and pageantry yet remain in the form of the actual masks used in those ancient dances. In the National Museums are 31 Gigaku masks of the seventh century from the temple Horyu-ji; 164 eighth-century masks are preserved in the Shoso-in and 28 more of the same period at Todai-ji, though some are dispersed; making an almost miraculous number of 223 seventh- and eighth-century masks still in existence, a total which can surely be matched nowhere else in the world.

Most of these masks were carved from wood and then painted, although a few were painted on a base of successive layers of linen cloth and lacquer. One is immediately struck by how much larger Gigaku masks are than most other masks. This is because they were made to cover the entire head, or at least a large part of it, rather than the face only. Both their large size and the deep carving also served to heighten their effect when used in the open air, where Gigaku performances took place.

Although it seems fairly well established by tradition that Gigaku came to Japan from central China, neither old masks nor anything similar to Gigaku can be found in China today. Much farther west, however, in ancient Greece, somewhat similar masks seem to have been used in the festivals of Bacchus, god of wine, later developing into the masks of Grecian drama. No one is ever likely to find a direct connection between the masks of Ancient Greece and those of the Japanese Gigaku, but the fact remains that Alexander did invade India and that we know Grecian wine was imported in the ancient Chinese capital of Changan. Also, the Brahman character in Gigaku definitely suggests Indian influences, so some connection with Ancient Greece is not beyond the realm of possibility. As we know, civilization has had an amazing way of spreading along valleys, over mountains, and even across deserts. The masked dances of Lamaism have several similarities to Gigaku, suggesting that they both may have derived from a common source.

Bugaku

It was the great popularity of the rival form Bugaku, imported from China somewhat later, that finally put an end to Gigaku. Bugaku itself is so complex that no adequate exposition of its content can be attempted here. It consists mainly of dances performed both with and without masks. As it is still performed today, it has been often described.

The form reached its full development in China during the T'ang dynasty in the seventh and eighth centuries. According to contemporary records, the T'ang emperors, expanding their territories and creating the great centralized culture of T'ang China, collected together as Bugaku the rare and curious music of fourteen countries and the dancing techniques of eight countries. It was these forms collected and perfected by the T'ang court that were introduced one after another into Japan during the Nara period (645–794) and account for the formal division of Japanese Bugaku into styles whose names indicate the regions from which the T'ang court collected the dances, e.g., Togaku (China), Koraigaku (Korea), Shiragigaku (Korea), Bokkaigaku (Manchuria), Tenjikugaku (India), Rinyugaku (Indo-China), and the like. Taking all these styles together, Bugaku was incomparably richer in both form and content than was Gigaku. Whereas the emphasis in Gigaku was on the comic and even the ribald, Bugaku consisted largely of refined and complex dances.

Since rhythmic beauty is essential in all dances, a complex musical idiom was needed for Bugaku, and this in turn led to an increase in the types of musical instruments used. Gigaku had made use of only three instruments—*fue* (flute), *dohatsu* (bronze gong), and *koshi-tsutsumi* (hip drum). Bugaku enlarged the orchestra to include three types of drums (*taiko, dadaiko,* and *kekko*), the *fue* (flute), *sho* (a circular panpipe), *shichiriki* (flageolet-like reed instrument), *koto* (zither-like harp), *biwa* (lute), and *kugo* (23-string harp). Whereas in Gigaku the music was performed in a moving procession and hence the instruments had to be small and portable, Bugaku provided a formal stage for the dancers with places for the orchestra to sit on either side, so the larger instruments could be used.

When compared with Bugaku, Gigaku came to seem most simple and even rustic. Little wonder then that, at first in the imperial court and gradually even in the great temples, the more gorgeous and entertaining new form gradually supplanted the older. By the Heian period (794–1185) Bugaku had reached its full flowering and was greatly developed and refined by its great popularity among court circles, the nobles competing in performing its music and dances as part of the court culture; it is this Heian-period Bugaku which still exists today, regular performances being given not only at the imperial court in Tokyo, but at several of the larger shrines and temples.

As for the masks of Bugaku, they have three outstanding characteristics: they are symbolic rather than realistic in expression; they are small and light; and they have movable parts. Gigaku masks were much more realistic, as the Gigaku performance was more dramatic in content. Bugaku, on the other hand, expressed human actions by abstract rhythmic motions; hence the masks quite correctly avoided excessive realism and tended, by means of appropriate exaggeration or simplification, toward the symbolic, as for example in the decoratively carved wrinkles of Ranryo-o *(Plate 2)* and Nasori *(Plate 24)* and the beautiful arches of the mouth and eyebrows of Chikyu *(Plate 25)* and Shintoriso *(Plate 3)*. In the matter of weight, Bugaku masks, covering only the face, were much smaller and lighter than those of Gigaku and more appropriate for the greater activity of the Bugaku dance. The lack of a back-piece required great lightness in order to keep them in place. Fortunately, by that time Japanese sculpture was well developed and was able to produce masks that were not only thin and light but also possessed true artistic excellence. Even the Ranryo-o mask, despite its elaborate dragon decoration, is not nearly so heavy as it appears, every detail being finely worked out with the greatest of delicacy.

The technique of moving eyes and chin is found in no other Japanese masks. It is true that some of the many categories of Bugaku do not use masks with movable parts, but most of

3 舞楽 新鳥蘇
法隆寺蔵 12 世紀
BUGAKU MASK: SHINTORISO.
12th century.
Hōryūji Temple, Nara.

them do. For example the masks of Ranryo-o, Nasori, and Saisoro have eyes that move up and down and mouths that open and shut. The nose of Kotokuraku *(Plate 19)* sways right and left, Bato's *(Plate 8)* hair can be put in motion, and Genjoraku *(Plate 23)* has vertically moving cheeks, which produce the illusion of the eyes and mouth opening and closing. These various parts must depend upon manual manipulation and are consequently somewhat mechanical, but their rhythmical motions still manage to produce a peculiarly unrealistic beauty all their own.

Among the various Bugaku masks there are some that resemble masks found in distant Ceylon and Java, a fact which suggests that at least some of the Bugaku dances came originally from lands far beyond China, but it is now no longer possible to trace such derivations with any historical accuracy. Most of the masks now extant date from the eleventh to fourteenth centuries, whereas Bugaku had reached its height during the eighth to twelfth centuries. As early as the year 752 both Gigaku and several different forms of Bugaku were performed with much splendor at the unveiling of the great image of Buddha in the Todai-ji. Doubtlessly, the masks used in those earliest days were worn out through use in successive centuries, so rather than lament their loss we should be happy with the few remaining examples from the eleventh century. As a general rule, the older the mask, the more artistic its execution. Although Bugaku has survived until today, the declining powers of its aristocratic patronage during the medieval centuries of military rule seem to have been reflected directly in a decline in the artistry of the Bugaku mask.

Gyodo

Gyodo is a Buddhist term for a ceremony which still exists in Japan today, being more commonly known as *neri-kuyo*. The ceremony consists of a procession in which some holy image, ordinarily kept unseen in a temple or shrine, is carried through the streets exposed to the people, thereby bathing their minds in the virtues of the god represented. This was a widespread practice in T'ang China and was introduced to Japan along with Buddhism in the Nara period. Although originally a Buddhist ceremony, it was soon adopted by the Shinto shrines and is today more Shinto than Buddhist in practice. Nevertheless, it is still occasionally performed as a Buddhist cremony upon the opening of a new temple, and traces of the practice yet remain in ceremonies at such ancient temples as Horyu-ji and Taima-ji.

The Shoryo ceremony of Horyu-ji, said to date from the Nara period, consists of a procession about the temple precincts bearing the ashes and a statue of Shotoku Taishi in a highly decorated palanquin, and the masks which the palanquin bearers wear are known as Gyodo masks. In those hierarchical days of the ceremony's inception, it was considered inappropriate for such sacred burdens to be carried on the shoulders of ordinary coolies, and the bearers' faces were accordingly hidden by masks representing the Eight Bushu, the attendants of Buddha, thereby doubtlessly enhancing the effect of the procession in the eyes of its beholders. It is also recorded that twelve attendants wearing masks of the Twelve Deva Kings bore the sacred palanquin at the memorial ceremony of the pagoda at Kyo-o Gokoku-ji in the year 1086, and some of the masks used on that occasion still remain. Most Gyodo masks represent such Buddhist guardians as the Eight Bushu, the Twenty-eight Bushu, and the Twelve Deva Kings, but

4 舞楽 皇仁帝
東大寺蔵 11 世紀
BUGAKU MASK:
ONINTEI.
11th century.
Tōdaiji Temple, Nara.

the processions were generally led by persons wearing masks of Tengu (long-nosed goblins, corresponding to the Gigaku Chido) and Shishi (lions, *Plate 31)*, who added still further dignity to the procession.

There was another sort of Gyodo, in which religious scenes were re-enacted. An old record recounts that in 861, upon the repairing of the head of the Great Buddha at Todai-ji, characters representing the Buddhist deities Fugen-bosatsu *(Plate 26)*, Karyo-binga, Tamon-ten, Kichijo-ten, and Daijizai-ten, accompanied by 14 devils, 20 heavenly maidens, and 60 celestial beings, appeared on the stage and enacted scenes of worshiping and making offerings to Buddha. This is one of the oldest records of a dramatic presentation, and there is every reason to assume the characters wore masks.

This type of Gyodo still survives in the Raigo ceremony of the Jodo (Pure Land) sect. When in the tenth century the high-ranking priest Eshin began to preach the new Pure Land doctrine, saying that Buddha in his mercy would come down from paradise with his saints to redeem all those who had had faith in Amida Buddha, ruler of the Pure Land, a great number of pictures were produced representing this scene and, to make it even more understandable to the common people, pageants were presented in the temple grounds. This was the Raigo ceremony (also called *mukaeko*), which soon spread to many localities and is still performed at Taima-ji in Yamato and Kuho-ji in Kanto. The pageant consists of a procession of actors wearing the masks of Buddhist saints and escorting a statue of the Buddha across a long, narrow passage connecting two separate buildings in the temple compound.

In Gyodo there is no great movement, and its masks also are quiet and rather featureless, most of them being mere reproductions of the countenances of Buddhist statues. The eyes are open to permit the wearers to see, but the mouths are generally closed. Being imitative and static in quality, they are not so interesting as masks, but the Raigo ceremony became so popular and diffused througout the nation that a number of the masks still remain in various localities.

Tsuina

The Tsuina ceremony, as it still exists today, consists of the scattering of beans to drive out devils on the eve of the first day of spring. The custom was imported during the Nara period from China, where it had existed since the Chou dynasty (1122–249 B.C.). The ceremony was at first performed only in the imperial court, but the practice soon spread to the temples and finally, in a much simpler form, to private houses throughout the land.

In the early Tsuina, the character who drove out the evil spirits, called Hososhi, was the one who wore the four-eyed, grotesque mask and brandished a halberd, but in time the mask came to be worn by the devil himself, and today the Tuina mask is definitely a devil mask. Some say that the mask passed from the devil-subduer to the devil because it had such a fierce expression that people gradually came to feel it would be more appropriate for a devil. But a more likely explanation is that in the earliest ceremonies the devil did not appear, being regarded as invisible spirits, and that when an actual devil was desired for a more exciting and dramatic performance, he was given the only mask which the ceremony possessed. Today the ceremony consists of little more than some member of a household scattering beans to

5 追儺鬼 法隆寺蔵
13 世紀
TSUINA MASK: ONI (Demon). 13th century.
Hōryūji Temple, Nara

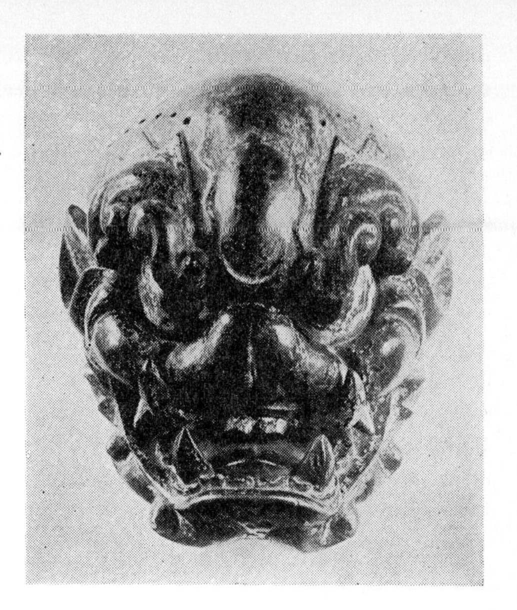

the four corners of the principal room and reciting the verse "Drive bad luck out, let good luck in."

A large number of old Tsuina masks still exist, bearing witness to how widespread the custom was in Japan. Some of them come in pairs, representing a devil-husband and devil-wife or devil-father and devil-son. As these masks were not used for any complex drama, the only need was for a mask representing the fearful defeat of a fierce devil, and the makers stretched their imaginations to the limit in this regard. In some ways they are similar in purpose and appearance to the Konron mask of Gigaku *(Plate 15)*, but they are richer in variety, developing to the point of distinguishing between male and female demons, between old and young demons.

Noh

The fourteenth century witnessed the perfection of the Noh mask, undoubtedly, in its profound and refined expression, one of the finest dramatic masks the world has ever seen. These masterpieces did not, however, simply spring into being overnight. They had a long tradition behind them in the masks of Gigaku, Bugaku, and Gyodo—rich and deep underground streams flowing throughout the country and finally meeting in a glorious confluence and bursting forth into light as the masks of Noh and Kyogen. The definitive history of the development of the Noh and the Noh mask is yet to be written, but it seems fairly well established that the Noh grew out of such dances as those called Dengaku and Sarugaku, both of which used crude masks. A few of these early masks still remain, and the Okina mask of the Noh, with all the sacred tradition behind it, doubtless retains much of the Dengaku character. But, first and foremost the development of this great mask must be credited to the development of Noh itself and to those two great geniuses of the Noh and founders of the Kanze school, Kanami (1333–84) and his son Zeami (1363–1444).

During the Heian period collateral branches or offshoots of the great traditional families of court musicians were entertaining the common people with dances and music, more or less dramatic in content, called Dengaku and Sarugaku. Although somewhat rustic in feeling, these performances, in contrast with the stately dances of the imperial court and the temples, gave unreserved expression to the feelings of the masses and were proving tremendously popular. Seeing how the people enjoyed this mimicry, Kanami and Zeami refined it greatly and gave it true dramatic value, adding to it the graceful melodies and forms of the Shirabyoshi dances which were then popular among the nobility. The result was such a tremendous success that it finally attracted the interest of the military ruler of the nation, the shogun Yoshimitsu, under whose patronage Noh achieved the fully developed form in which we know it today. One of the great achievements of Noh was that it cleansed itself of the mimicry and buffoonery which had characterized its predecessors, relegating this element of low comedy to the Kyogen, of which we shall speak next, and emerged as a refined and predominantly tragic form, achieving "gaiety in subtlety," as the saying goes. Masks were developed in keeping with the spirit and greatness of this new form.

Let us briefly summarize the outstanding characteristics of the Noh mask. First, it is a mask of tragedy. No other mask has ever been made which so fittingly expresses the fate and the emotions of the tragic hero. Second, as it must be worn for a long time in a complex plot, its size and weight has been reduced to the absolute minimum. Third, it has a neutral expression, permitting it to express the many emotions of its part during the course of the play. Far, however, from being expressionless, it is a mask which, on the face of a great actor, can assume numerous expressions—an upward tilt of the head to catch the light, and it is a happy, "shining" mask; long shadows as it is turned downward, and it is a sad, "cloudy" face. Fourth, since Noh developed from mimicry, its mask is somewhat realistic, but never too much so, reality always being subdued to the appreciation of the abstract beauty of the human face, to the principle of "gaiety in subtlety." Fifth, it is the work of a specialist, of a Noh-mask carver called a *men-uchi*. The earlier masks of Gigaku, Bugaku, and Gyodo had been the spare-time handiwork of the carvers of Buddhist statues, and many of them indeed reflect the great ability of their carvers. But the Noh mask required more than artistic ability: it demanded a profound understandnig of the complex nature of Noh itself, of the use to which each mask would be put. Only a specialist could fill this need, and the *men-uchi* appeared. The masks they carved were so perfectly fitted to their purposes as to be called the perfect products of true artistic genius.

The so-called "ten master carvers" of Noh masks lived, in all likelihood, about the time of Kanami and Zeami, as the perfection of the Noh drama and the Noh mask went hand in hand. These were Nikko, Miroku, Yasha, Fukuhara Bunzo, Ishikawa Tatsuemon, Akazuru Yoshinari, Himi Munetada, Echi Yoshifune, Koushi Kiyomitsu, and Tokuwaka Tadamasa. After them the art of mask carving became divided into different schools; the masters of this period were Zoami, Fukurai, Haruwaka, Horai, Chigusa, and Sankobo. By the beginning of the seventeenth century the forms of Noh had become fixed and newly carved masks were nothing but imitations, skillful or not, of the older masks. Until the modern era the Noh continued to enjoy the support and patronage of the military aristocracy and flourished greatly as the entertainment of the samurai. The principal makers of Noh masks in this later period were the families of Izeki, Ono-deme, and Echizen-deme, all descended from Sankobo.

Noh masks are divided into the five categories—gods, men, women, insane persons, and demons—which categories are, in

6 能 顰 15 世紀
奈良国立博物館蔵
NOH MASK: SHIKAMI.
15th century. *Nara National Museum.*

turn, variously subdivided. Gods such as Tenjin, Beshimi, and Tobide *(Plate 39)* are represented with nonhuman masks, but other gods who appear on the stage in the guise of old men use appropriate human masks. The masks of men include about ten varieties, young and old, humble and noble, those for such tragic heroes as Yorimasa, Kagekiyo *(Plate 38)*, Shunkan, and Yowahoshi being particularly excellent. As all Noh parts are played by men, all players of female roles must be masked and the female mask is of great importance. These female masks not only indicate whether the character is young or old, humble or noble, but are also carefully carved to bring out the particular beauty of each type, whether it be that of the young and virginal or of the middle-aged and worried. Being a drama of tragedy, Noh shows many persons who have lost their minds through grief or jealousy, and great attention is given to their masks; particularly striking examples are the gruesome yet somehow beautiful Masukami-ouna and the stingingly grim Hannya *(Plate 33)*.

Noh masks of the earliest period are occasionally preserved in old shrines and temples. Those of the great makers have been largely preserved in the great families of Noh performers. The later, imitative masks have been preserved mainly in the families descended from the feudal lords who were the patrons of Noh. Much has been said and written about the makers of these various masks, but, except for the more recent examples, the actual fact is that it is practically impossible to speak with any accuracy of the authorship of the earlier masks.

Kyogen

The sister arts of Noh and Kyogen are actually but two sides of a single art, Noh being the tragic and Kyogen the comic. A typical present-day Noh performance consists of five Noh plays, divided by three comic interludes of Kyogen, both the tragic and the comic elements being heightened in effect by the resulting contrasts. The great popularity of Dengaku and Sarugaku was certainly due to the comical element. While the innovators of the Noh were wise in eradicating this element from their tragic dramas, they were also wise in not discarding it entirely, but keeping it as a necessary adjunct to the new form. Thus Noh and Kyogen reinforce each other and the comic quality of the Kyogen has been greatly refined and sharpened along with the development of the Noh.

The libretto of the Noh is both highly poetical and literary, while that of the Kyogen is colloquial. Action on the Noh stage is accompanied by the chanting of either the actors or the chorus, while the Kyogen actors speak all their own lines. Noh action is dance, while that of Kyogen is broad gesture and mimicry. And just as the two forms contrast in these particulars, so do their masks stand out in sharp contrast with each other.

To briefly summarize the characteristics of the Kyogen mask, it is, in the first place, frank and outspoken where the Noh mask is subtle and profound. Secondly, whereas the Noh mask seeks for the neutral expression, the Kyogen mask expresses but a single quality, be it anger or laughter or naivety. Thirdly, while Noh masks usually represent noble or beautiful faces, the faces of Kyogen are those of the common man, frequently in his uglier aspects. Finally, the variety and classification of Kyogen masks is not so complex as with those of Noh, as the same mask is used for many different plays.

Kyogen masks may be divided into two groups. First there are the happily or foolishly smiling masks, tempting the audience to smile with them. And then there are the non-smiling masks which induce lauhgter by some comical element of contradiction. They may also be classified into the same five categories of the Noh mask—gods, men, women, insane persons, and demons—but since their uses are not so specialized, there are actually only about twenty different kinds of Kyogen masks. The god masks represent such happy, smiling gods of good luck as Ebisu and Daikoku *(Plate 42)*, and those of men are of good-humored samurai or ordinary citizens. None of the Kyogen women are particularly beautiful, but their ugliness always has a certain risible charm and is never disgusting. Since Kyogen eschews the tragic, there are no real insane characters in it and this class of masks is reserved rather for ghosts, ghosts which are comical and not at all frightening, as for example that of the young man about town who cannot enter Nirvana because he is so passionately devoted to playing the flute. The demon masks likewise are comical rather than frightening, many showing the faces of such animals as the monkey *(Plate 44)*, the fox, or the cow. There is also the Usobuki mask, with its pouting lips, which may represent the spirit of such diverse creatures as a cicada, an octopus, an ant, or even a mosquito, while the Kentoku mask represents the spirit of a crab, a sparrow, or a silver carp. Thus Kyogen masks have an extremely wide range of use, a fact which accounts for their lack of variety.

It is generally believed that the old Kyogen masks were made by the same hands as those which carved the masks of the Noh. There is no way to prove this tradition, but it is easy to believe that the same skill which produced the Noh masterpieces could well have produced these lighter pieces. The old masks, outside of a few in shrines and temples, are now mainly found in the old families of Kyogen actors.

As we have seen, the masks of the Noh and Kyogen were produced under the patronage of the military class, but they also had their more popular counterparts in the masks used in Kagura, the popular dances still staged in shrines and temples throughout the country. These Kagura masks, however, are more interesting ethnologically than artistically, being in the main but debased examples of Noh and Kyogen masks.

7 伎楽 迦楼羅 東大寺蔵 8 世紀
GIGAKU-MASK; KARURA. 8th century.
Tōdaiji Temple, Nara.

8 舞楽　抜頭　厳島神社蔵　12 世紀
BUGAKU-MASK ; BATŌ. 12th century.
Itsukushima Shrine, Hiroshima.

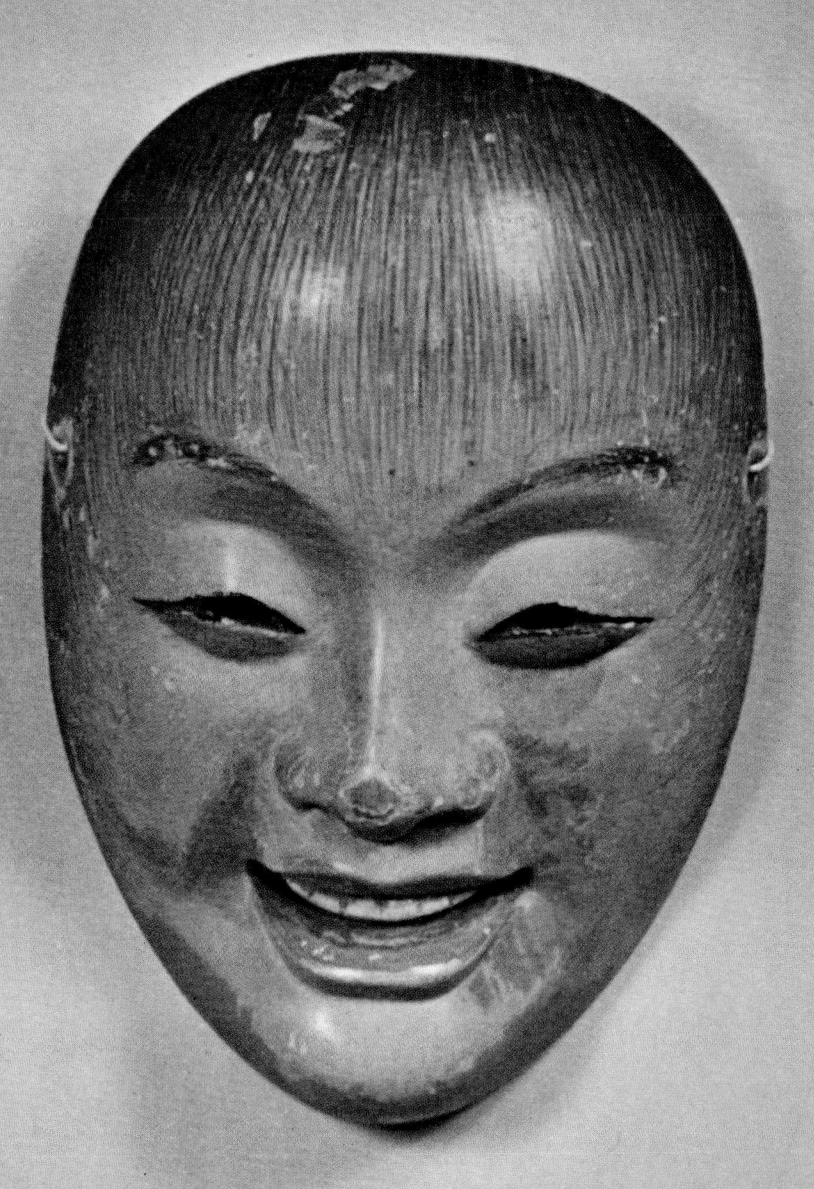

9 能 猩々 奈良国立博物館蔵 15 世紀
NOH-MASK; SHŌJŌ. 15th century.
Nara National Museum.

10
伎楽　力士　東京国立博物館蔵　7世紀
GIGAKU-MASK; RIKISHI. 7th century.
Tokyo National Museum.

11
伎楽　呉公　東京国立博物館蔵　7世紀
GIGAKU-MASK; GOKŌ. 7th century.
Tokyo National Museum.

12 伎楽 波羅門 東大寺蔵 8 世紀
GIGAKU MASK: BARAMON (Brahman)
8th century. *Tōdaiji Temple, Nara.*

13 伎楽 獅子児 東大寺蔵 8 世紀
GIGAKU-MASK; SHISHIKO. 8th century.
Tōdaiji Temple, Nara.

14 伎楽　治道　東京国立博物館蔵　7 世紀
GIGAKU-MASK; CHIDŌ. 7th century.
Tokyo National Museum.

15 伎楽 崑崙 東大寺蔵 8 世紀
GIGAKU-MASK; KONRON. 8th century.
Tōdaiji Temple, Nara.

16 伎楽　呉女　正倉院蔵　8 世紀
GIGAKU-MASK; GOJO. 8th century.
Shōsōin Temple, Nara.

17 伎楽　酔胡従　東京国立博物館蔵　7 世紀
GIGAKU-MASK ; SUIKOJŪ. 7th century.
Tokyo National Museum.

18 伎楽　酔胡王　東京国立博物館蔵　8 世紀
GIGAKU-MASK; SUIKO-Ō. 8th century.
Tokyo National Museum.

19 舞楽 胡徳楽 手向山神社蔵 12 世紀
BUGAKU-MASK; KOTOKURAKU. 12th century.
Tamukeyama Shrine, Nara.

20 舞楽 崑崙八仙 手向山神社蔵 12 世紀
BUGAKU-MASK; KOROBASE. 12th century.
Tamukeyama Shrine, Kyoto.

21 舞楽 二ノ舞（尉） 厳島神社蔵 12 世紀
BUGAKU-MASK; NINOMAI, (Jō). 12th century
Itsukushima Shrine, Hiroshima.

22 舞楽 二ノ舞（嫗） 厳島神社蔵 12 世紀
BUGAKU-MASK; NINOMAI, (Ouna). 12th century.
Itsukushima Shrine, Hiroshima.

23 舞楽 還城楽 厳島神社蔵 12 世紀
BUGAKU-MASK; GENJŌRAKU. 12th century.
Itsukushima, Shrine, Hiroshima.

24 舞楽 納蘇利 厳島神社蔵 12 世紀
BUGAKU-MASK ; NASORI. 12th century.
Itsukushima Shrine, Hiroshima.

25 舞楽 地久 手向山神社蔵 11 世紀
BUGAKU-MASK ; CHIKYŪ. 11th, century.
Tamukeyama Shrine, Nara.

26 行道 菩薩 東大寺蔵 12 世紀

GYŌDO-MASK; BOSATSU. 12th century.

Tōdaiji Temple, Nara.

27 行道 輿舁（乾闥婆） 法隆寺蔵 12 世紀

GYŌDŌ-MASK ; KOSHIKAKI, (Kandatsuba). 12th century.

Hōryūji Temple Nara.

28 行道 火天 教王護国寺蔵 10世紀
GYŌDŌ-MASK; KATEN. 10th century.
Kyō-ō Gokokuji Temple, Kyoto.

29 行道 八部衆（鳩槃荼） 教王護国寺蔵 12世紀
GYŌDŌ-MASK; HACHIBUSHŪ, (Kubanda).
12th century. *Kyō-ō Gokokuji Temple, Kyoto.*

30 行道 鬼 押立神社蔵 16 世紀
GYŌDŌ-MASK; ONI (demon). 16th century.
Oshitate Shrine, Shiga.

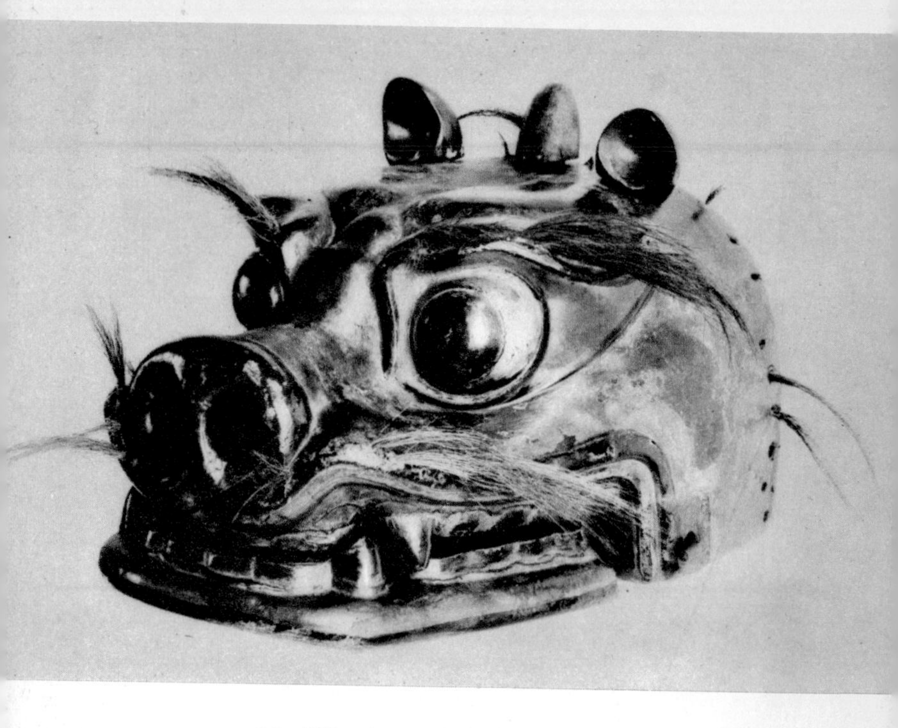

31 行道 獅子 法隆寺蔵 12 世紀
GYŌDŌ-MASK; SHISHI. 12th century.
Hōryūji Temple, Nara.

32 追儺 鬼 法隆寺蔵 13 世紀
TSUINA-MASK; ONI (demon). 13th century.
Hōryūji Temple, Nara.

33 能 般若 三井高公氏蔵 14 世紀
NOH-MASK ; HANNYA. 14th century.
Mitsui Collection, Tokyo.

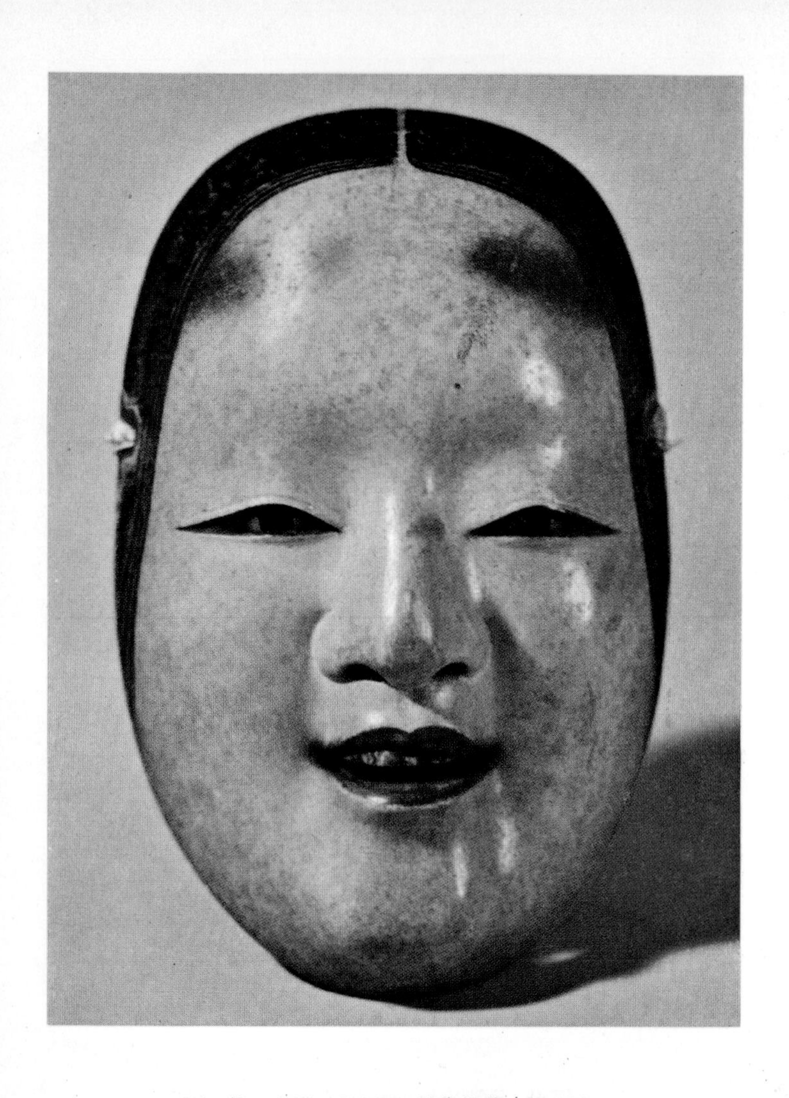

34 能 小面 東京国立博物館蔵 15 世紀
NOH-MASK; KO-OMOTE. 15th century.
Tokyo National Museum.

35 能　翁（白式尉）　前田利建氏蔵
15 世紀

NOH-MASK; OKINA, (Hakushikijō)
15th century, *Maeda Collection, Tokyo.*

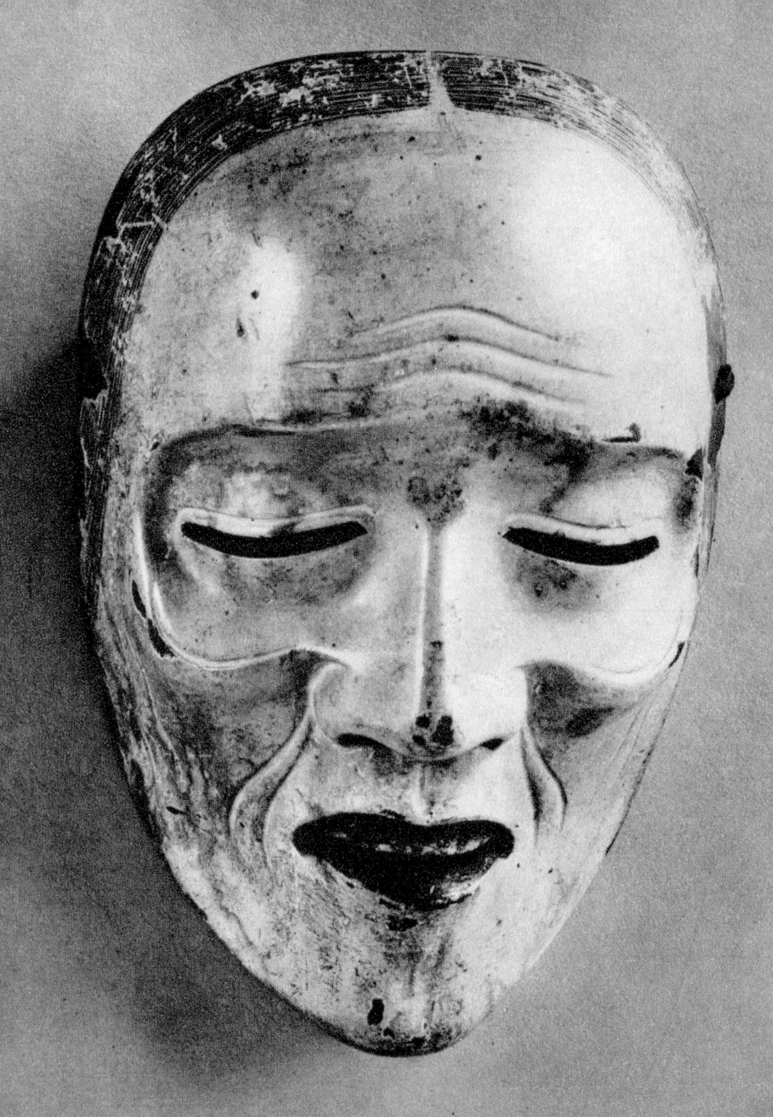

36 能 姥 宝生家蔵 15 世紀
NOH-MASK; UBA. 15th century.
Hōshō Collection, Tokyo.

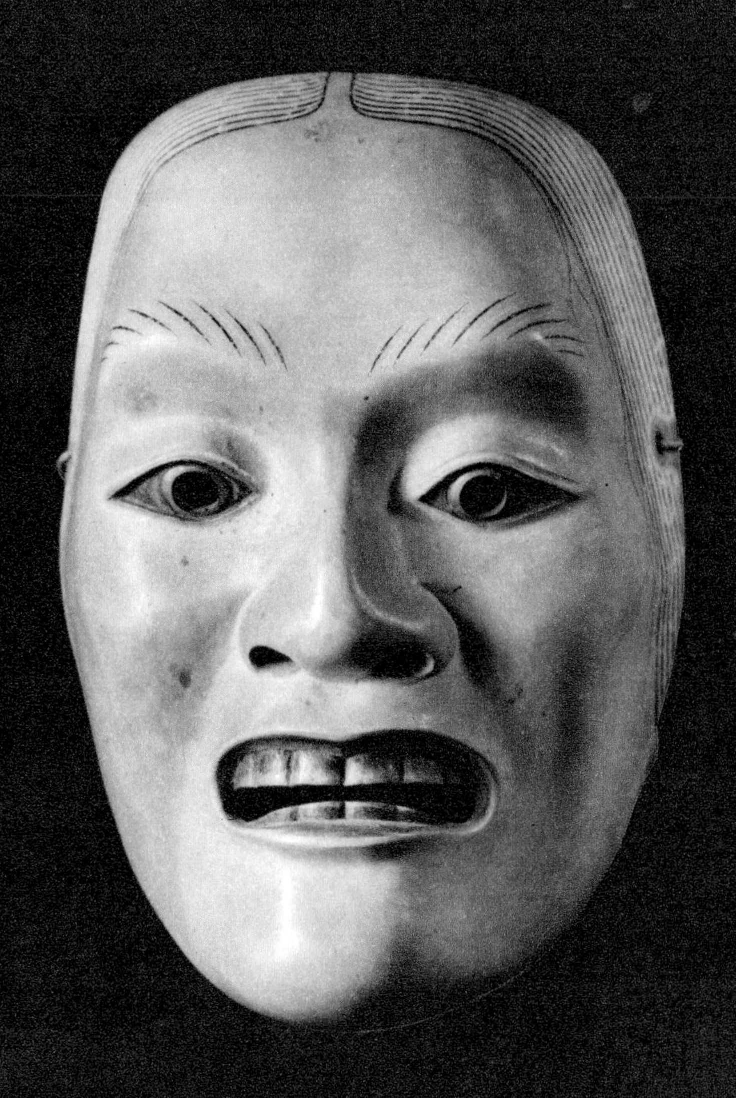

37 能　山姥　東京国立博物館蔵　16 世紀
NOH-MASK; YAMAUBA. 16th century.
Tokyo National Museum.

38 能 景清 東京国立博物館蔵 17 世紀
NOH-MASK; KAGEKIYO. 17th century.
Tokyo National Museum.

39 能　猿飛出　奈良国立博物館蔵　16 世紀
NOH-MASK; SARUTOBIDE. 16th century.
Nara National Museum.

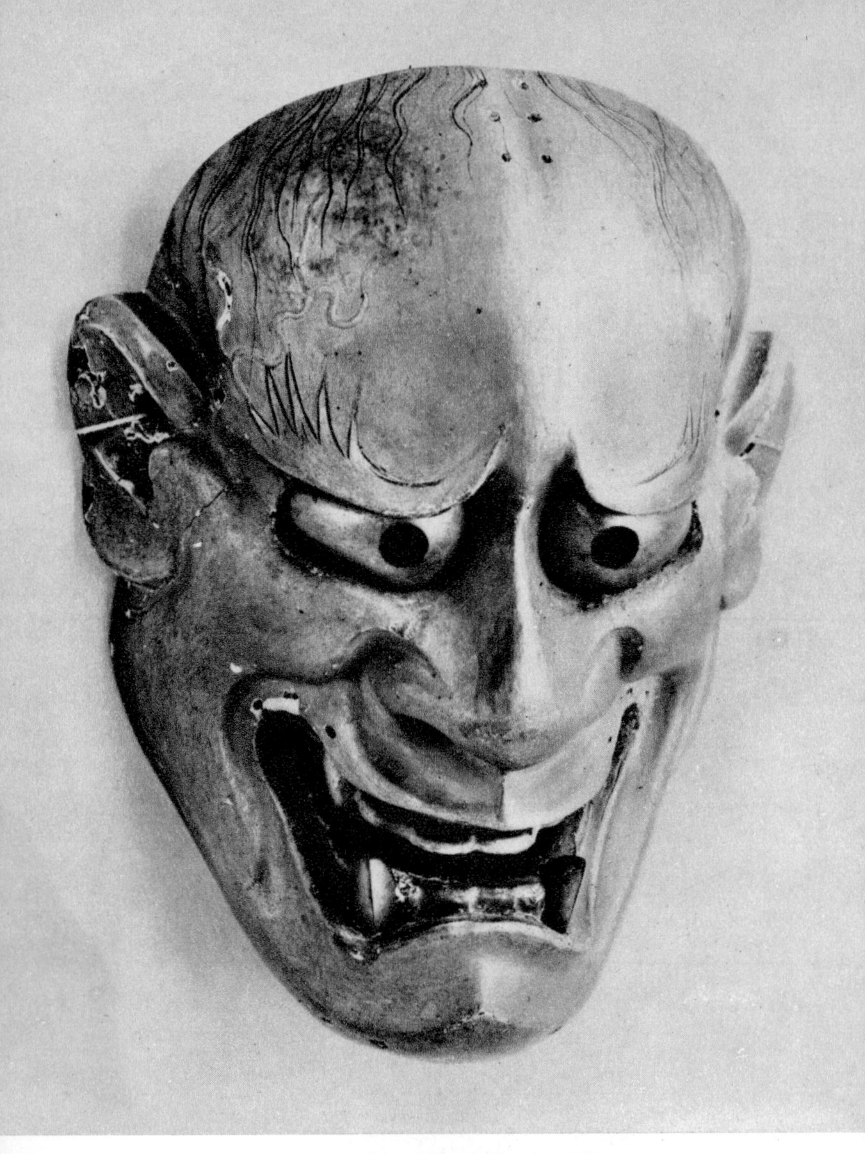

40 能 泥蛇 観世家蔵 14 世紀
NOH-MASK; DEIJA. 14th century.
Kanze Collection, Tokyo.

41 狂言　乙　東京国立博物館蔵　15 世紀
KYŌGEN-MASK ; OTO. 15th century.
Tokyo National Museum.

42 狂言 大黒 東京国立博物館蔵 16 世紀
KYŌGEN-MASK; DAIKOKU. 16th century.
Tokyo National Museum.

43 狂言 賢徳 東京国立博物館蔵 16 世紀
KYOGEN-MASK; KENTOKU. 16th century.
Tokyo National Museum.

44 狂言　猿　東京国立博物館蔵　17 世紀

KYŌGEN-MASK; SARU (monkey). 17th century.

Tokyo National Museum.

45 狂言 登髭 東京国立博物館蔵 17 世紀

KYŌGEN-MASK; NOBORIHIGE. 17th century.

Tokyo National Museum.

46 狂言 小武悪 東京国立博物館蔵 15 世紀
KYŌGEN-MASK; KOBUAKU. 15th century.
Tokyo National Museum.

Comments on the Plates

1. GIGAKU MASK: TAIKOFU. This mask was used at the unveiling of the Great Buddha at Todai-ji, in Nara, in 752. The character Taikofu is a lonely, disconsolate old man, and his presence in the Gigaku performance is probably a vestige of the elders who used to give benediction in prehistorical tribal ceremonies. However this may be, in the Gigaku the general effect of the mask and the old man's tottering gait was undoubtedly a comical one. Having been carved at a time when the art of sculpture was already well developed, this mask is most successful in the realistic expression of old age. There is something about the features which is definitely non-Japanese, suggesting that it was a copy of a foreign mask. The hair in eyebrows and whiskers has doubtless been replaced through the centuries, but probably in the original form.

2. BUGAKU MASK: RANRYO-O. This mask came from an ancient Indian drama, and similar masks are still found in Java. In China there is a legend that at the time of the Northern Ch'i dynasty there was a handsome young prince named Ranryo who was always victorious in battle because he wore such a mask as this; a dance using this mask has been long performed in Japan. The dragon crest is most imposing, and the rolling eyeballs and movable chin create a strong impression of rhythmic beauty.

3. BUGAKU MASK: SHINTORISO. The name of this mask means "new Toriso," as contrasted with another mask called "old Toriso," but the significance of the name is lost. According to tradition, these masks came to Japan with the Bugaku dances in the Korean or Manchurian styles, but since very similar masks exist in Java, it seems more likely that the masks originated in the South Seas. Of all remaining Bugaku masks, this is the most stylized, with its curving eyes and eyebrows, exaggerated mustache and red spots on the cheeks. In a way it is reminiscent of the European Pierrot, which of course may be only coincidental. The mask is worn in group dances of four or six dancers.

4. BUGAKU MASK: ONINTEI. This mask is used in a majestic and auspicious dance in which four or six dancers participate, wearing magnificent crowns. It is traditionally said to be a copy of the mask worn by Wani of the Korean kingdom Kudara when he danced at the coronation of Emperor Nintoku in the year 313. However that may be, the mask is evocative of magnificent pageantry at the court of a Chinese emperor, thronged with envoys from all the nations of Asia. The eyes, eyebrows, and mouth are quite stylized, and the solemn visage is one befitting some foreign ambassador. The date 1042 is carved in this particular example.

5. TSUINA MASK: ONI (Demon). This is a Tsuina demon used in the bean-throwing ceremony at Horyu-ji, in which three demons—father, mother, and son—are driven out by the god Bishamon. Temple tradition identifies the mask here illustrated as that of the son, but it has more of the characteristics of a mother-demon. In any case it is difficult to distinguish age and sex in such masks. The heavy, strong lines of this example indicate that it was carved in the Kamakura period (1185–1333), which makes it one of the oldest Tsuina masks remaining to us.

6. NOH MASK: SHIKAMI. This mask is aptly called Shikami, meaning "grimace." It is worn in the Noh by such angry gods as Shari or Raiden or by such evil spirits as Oeyama, Rashomon, or Tsuchigumo. This shows masculine sturdiness as contrasted with the feminine viciousness of Hannya *(Plate 33)* and Deija *(Plate 40)*, male anger being explicitly stated and female anger being only implied.

7. GIGAKU MASK: KARURA. In Indian mythology, Karura is the sacred bird which feeds on poisonous snakes. Entering the Buddhist pantheon, the bird became one of the Eight Bushu, the guardians of Buddha. The Karura part in the Gigaku dance is described in the *Kyokunsho* as a *soshumai* (quick-hands dance), which identifies it as a lively, bird-like part. The unobtrusive carving of this mask makes it worthy of the Nara-period sculpture, and it is also outstanding in that it still retains some of its original colors.

8. BUGAKU MASK: BATO. The prototype of this mask is believed to have been brought to Japan either by a Brahman priest who came from India during the Nara period or by Buttetsu, a Buddhist priest from Indo-China; in Bugaku it has been classified with the Indian style of dance. Recent research says the mask derives from a mythological Indian tale concerning a white horse who kills a poisonous snake. In China and Japan, however, the mask is said to represent the anger of a son whose father has been killed by wild beasts, or the face of an empress whose burning jealousy has turned her into a demon. Whatever its origin, the dance in which this mask is used is very vigorous, with violent movements that are rare in Bugaku. Noteworthy are the parrot-beak nose, flying eyebrows, and the contrast of the dangling, dark-blue-hemp hair with the deep red of the face.

9. NOH MASK: SHOJO. Although the word *shojo* means orangoutang, here it is the name of a legendary Chinese fairy who lived on the banks of the Hsin-yang River and was a great tippler. The Noh dance performed by this fairy in search of wine is considered a propitious one. Although the mask has the cheerful features of a child and the ruddy flush of alcoholism, there is nevertheless the air of fairy-like mystery about it. Unlike the drunken dances of Gigaku and Bugaku, this does not depict the comedy of intoxication, but instead creates the imaginary world of a wine-thirsty fairy.

10. GIGAKU MASK: RIKISHI (Wrestler). Wrestlers of strong physique are regarded as Buddhist guardians, and powerful images of them often flank the entrances of Buddhist temples. The Rikishi of Gigaku was the bodyguard of a beautiful girl, who fought the ugly Konron when he made indecent advances to his mistress. This particular mask is a superb work of art, suggesting the sturdiness of the wrestler's entire body through his straining facial muscles.

11. GIGAKU MASK: GOKO. The name translates literally as "king of Go," Go being the ancient Chinese kingdom from which Gigaku was derived, but in the case of this mask the term means simply the king of some faraway land. With the elaborate crown and handsome features, it is a mask befitting a king. Contemporary records say the character wearing this mask appeared at the beginning of the Gigaku performance and played the role of a piper. This example is similar to the Shitenno mask of Horyu-ji both in carving technique and in being made of camphor wood, indicating that it is of great antiquity.

12. GIGAKU MASK: BARAMON (Brahman). The intellectual appearance of this mask is one befitting a Brahman, the high scholar-priest caste of India, and the headgear was also probably an indication of high caste. The contradiction between this stately mask and the comic part its wearer played in Gigaku doubtlessly heightened the audience's amusement: the serious scholar was frolicking about the stage, waving a long, white banner. His dance was called *mutsuki-arai,* "washing baby diapers," which certainly did nothing to lessen the comic effect.

13. GIGAKU MASK: SHISHIKO. Although the name of this mask might suggest a lion cub, actually it refers to a young boy who appeared on the Gigaku stage leading a lion, displaying his great abilities as a lion-tamer. Here the carver has been most successful in the difficult task of depicting both the smooth face of a boy and his bright, gay character. There is another juvenile Gigaku mask, that of the boy Taikoji, who accompanies the old Taikofu, and the two boys are somewhat difficult to tell apart, but there are subtle differences in coloration and expression.

14. GIGAKU MASK: CHIDO. Chido, meaning "road keeper," was the Gigaku character who served as a curtain-raiser, leading the procession onto the stage. The same long-nosed character was to appear later as the leader of the Gyodo procession, being there called Tengu or Sarudahiko. This example comes from Horyu-ji and is noteworthy for the technical excellence with which the carver has given the feeling of the skull beneath its flesh.

15. GIGAKU MASK: KONRON. Of all the Gigaku masks, this is the largest and most impressive. In early times the savages of the South Seas were called *konron,* but later the term was extended to apply to slaves and pagans in general. The Gigaku Konron, however, was a lustful creature who, as described previously (see the Gigaku section of the introduction), attempted to seduce the maiden of the following plate, creating great merriment by his silly, vulgar gestures and making a disheartened exit with his manhood broken off by the mighty wrestler of Plate 10. The bold, grand style of this mask is particularly impressive. Its weight was kept to a minimum by the use of paulownia wood.

16. GIGAKU MASK: GOJO (Maiden of Go). This mask of a maiden from the Chinese kingdom in which Gigaku originated is the only female Gigaku mask. The mask well expresses the purity and beauty of a young girl, while the coiffure is reminiscent of that found in other representations of noblewomen of ancient China. The serene cast of her mouth makes it likely that, despite her part opposite the comic Konron of the previous plate, her part was graceful and dignified rather than comic.

17. GIGAKU MASK: SUIKOJU. As the name suggests, this was the mask of one of the eight drunken attendants of the king Suiko *(Plate 18);* they appeared with their prince at the very end of the Gigaku performance and engaged in drunken buffoonery in a dance called *harameki,* a term which suggests that their bellies moved in and out in a most amusing way. Even in our own day the drunkard, losing all restraint and revealing his true nature, is the source of much amusement, and such a comic element was not overlooked in Gigaku. There each of the eight drunkards had his own distinguishing characteristics, not only of young and old but of the merry, or the maudlin, or the pugnacious drinker. The mask shown here is that of the merry drinker, and its terse carving has given the jovial drunkard an eternal intoxicated smile.

18. GIGAKU MASK: SUIKO-O (King Suiko). This is the king attended by the eight drunken attendants (see preceding paragraph), and the fact that he preserves his kingly dignity even in drunkenness must have made the antics of his attendants seem all the more boisterous. His name might be translated as "the drunken king of Persia," a derivation which seems to be corroborated by his distinctive features and the Persian-like shape of his headdress.

19. BUGAKU MASK: KOTOKURAKU. The Kotokuraku dance of Bugaku, performed by six dancers, is the counterpart of that danced in Gigaku by the Suikoju of Plate 17. Wine is served the six dancers by entertainers and waiters, and as they begin to dance and become merry, their long, hinged noses sway back and forth. Some, whose noses do not sway, complain that they haven't had enough to drink. This dance is not so vulgarly realistic as that of Gigaku evidently was, being a rhythmical suggestion of intoxication. The mask itself is stylized rather than realistic and the long, swaying noses, fastened at the top with a string, serve to emphasize the rhythmic beauty of the dance.

20. BUGAKU MASK: KOROBASE. This is an example of the masks worn by four dancers who wear green costumes and dance about in a circle representing the frolicsome movements of birds. The mask was originally green, with red eyes and mouth and a small bell hanging down from the beak to suggest the twittering of birds. Although most of the original color is now gone from this specimen, the very grain of the wood enhances the artistic effect.

21 & 22. BUGAKU NINOMAI MASKS: JO (Old Man) AND OUNA (Old Woman). The Ninomai, performed by a smiling, good-natured old man and his ugly wife, is much more realistic than most Bugaku dances. It is called Ninomai, "the second dance," because it always follows that called Amma, which is danced by two performers in full court dress and square cloth masks. The old couple watch the Amma dance and then, wishing to imitate it, try to borrow the dancers' wooden maces. When they are refused, they mount the stage without maces and perform a travasty of the preceding dance; this is the source of the Japanese expression "to perform the second dance," meaning to attempt an imitation which is beyond one's ability. There has been much conjecture about the origin of this dance, but little is known beyond the traditional view that it came from India. There are also quite similar Javanese masks.

23. BUGAKU MASK: GENJORAKU. Another name for this dance is Konjaraku, meaning "snake-viewing dance." In it several performers dance about an artificial serpent, supposedly depicting the joy of some snake-eating barbarians at the sight of their favorite food. The fact that it is often performed together with the Bato dance suggests the likelihood that it came from India. In time it came to be called by its present name, meaning "dance for the return of His Majesty," having been regarded as an auspicious dance to perform upon the return of an emperor to his palace. Mechanically, this is the most elaborate of Bugaku masks, being made in three moving parts—the eyebrows, forehead, and skull; the face proper, including the eyes and upper lip; and the lower face, including the teeth, with the chin attached by strings —the middle part, i.e., the face proper, being controlled by a string which the dancer holds in his teeth. When the face moves up under the forehead, as in the photograph, the eyes recede under the beetling brows and the mouth opens wide to reveal the teeth; when it moves down, the eyes appear much larger and the mouth becomes smaller. These mechanical movements emphasize the rhythm of the dance, but there is some difficulty in making the mask function smoothly.

24. BUGAKU MASK: NASORI. The Nasori is one of the older Bugaku dances and is frequently performed as a pair with the Ranryo. In Japan it has been traditionally regarded as of Korean origin, but actually it comes from an ancient Indian play called "Delight of the King," and similar masks are found in Java. Instead of the dragon which surmounts the Ranryo mask *(Plate 2)*, this has the large tusks to produce the ornamental effect and is a very typical Bugaku mask. The Nasori dance is performed sometimes by a single dancer and sometimes by two; in the latter case one mask is blue and the other green.

25. BUGAKU MASK: CHIKYU. The name of this dance, Chikyu, meaning "earth eternal," as well as the bright, shining expression of its mask has made this traditionally a most auspicious dance. It is performed by from four to six dancers. Although tradition classifies it in the Korean or Manchurian style, its actual origin is unknown. Since it resembles Shintoriso *(Plate 3)* in some ways, it also may have come from the South Seas; it should be noted, however, that the lines of Shintoriso are pictorial in their beauty, while those of Chikyu are sculptural. The mask here shown reveals this sculptural beauty of line to the full, having been carved in the closing years of the Heian period, when great emphasis was placed upon this quality.

26. GYODO MASK: BOSATSU (Bodhisattva). This is an example of the masks used in the Raigo ceremony of the Pure Land sect, depicting the advent of the Buddha Amida; the ceremony was popular in the late

Heian and the early Kamakura periods, and many of its masks are extant. This one from the Todai-ji is of considerable antiquity, being inscribed with the date of its donation, March 11, 1158, and is of great artistic excellence, even though, as all Gyodo masks were intended for pageantry and solemnity rather than dramatic use, it is quiet and almost featureless in effect.

27. GYODO MASK: KANDATSUBA. This is the mask of one of the eight bearers of the sacred palanquin in the Gyodo procession of the Shoryo ceremony at Horyu-ji; it represents Kandatsuba, one of the Eight Bushu who attended the Buddha. Except for its four eyes, this mask has the quiet, serene expression which characterizes all early Gyodo masks, whereas the later ones, such as those used at the Kyo-o Gokoku-ji *(Plate 29)*, are much more dynamic.

28. GYODO MASK: KATEN. The sacred palanquin used in the Gyodo procession at the memorial ceremony of the pagoda of the Kyo-o Gogoku-ji in 1086 was borne by twelve bearers masked to represent the Twelve Deva Kings, of which Katen is one. Seven of the original twelve masks are still preserved. Inscriptions on the back of the mask shown here indicate that it was mended twice, first in 1086 and again in 1334, and there is a record in the same temple to the effect that these masks were already in existence during the Choho era (999–1004). Their great antiquity is further authenticated by the facile and genial carving. The coloration probably dates from the mending of 1086.

29. GYODO MASK: KUBANDA. This mask represents one of the Eight Bushu and was made especially for the Gyodo memorial ceremony held at the pagoda of Kyo-o Gokoku-ji in 1334. This was the year of the Kemmu Restoration, in which the Hojo Regents were deposed and power restored to the emperor, and this calm and brilliant Gyodo ceremony was attended both by Emperor Godaigo, who would shortly be in flight to set up the ill-starred Southern Court, and by his vassal Ashikaga Takauji, who would set up his own candidate as emperor and make his own family the *de facto* rulers of Japan. This particular mask is much more decorative and powerful in expression—jocular even—than earlier examples of the same Eight Bushu *(see Plate 27)*. Doubtless, people were becoming tired of the too-quiet Gyodo mask and were turning from the religious to something more amusing. Although this development may have represented degeneration from the religious point of view, it did much to give Japanese masks a worldly liveliness.

30. GYODO MASK: ONI (Demon). Most of the demon masks now found in Japan are those used in the Tsuina ceremony *(Plates 5 & 32)*, but this example derives from the more primitive superstition which attributed disasters to the anger of demons and created masks and ceremonies for the appeasing of such anger. This primitive use of demon masks was revived in the Muromachi period (1392–1568), from which this mask dates, as Buddhism became neglected and the people reverted to native superstitions. In striking contrast to the Tsuina masks, these demon masks are most stylized, a quality which rose not to emphasize the rhythmic beauty of the dance as in Bugaku, but to symbolize demonhood. Thus the masks became quite formal, but they also had a considerable influence on the development of the Noh mask.

31. GYODO MASK: SHISHI (Lion). Lion masks were adopted in Gigaku, Gyodo, and, on special occasions, even in Bugaku. They are all quite similar in appearance, having been derived from the common source of the Shishi-mai or Lion Dance, which had a long and independent existence and is still performed today in many festivals throughout Japan. A number of Gigaku lion masks are preserved in the Shoso-in; no Bugaku examples remain, probably because the Lion Dance was never very popular there; among the remaining examples from Gyodo, that shown here is the oldest. Lion masks are quite large as they cover the entire head and also allow space for the manual opening and closing of the lower jaw. A large cloth is attached to the mask, covering the two persons who form the lion's body. In later years the carving of such masks became exaggerated and gaudy, attempting to show the lion's fearsomeness, but these older masks avoided such extremes, expressing rather the calm and dignity of the lion.

32. TSUINA MASK: ONI (Demon). This is a father-demon as contrasted with the smaller masks of mother-demons and son-demons *(see Plate 5)*. The carving here is indeed robust and masculine when compared with the other demon mask shown.

33. NOH MASK: HANNYA. Hannya is one of the greatest of all Noh masks and certainly the most fearsome. Representing the revengeful ghost of a once-beautiful woman, it is worn by the principal actor in the latter part of the plays "Aoi no Ue" and "Dojoji." The mask expresses the intensity of its resentment in its sunken, gilded eyes and its widespread mouth, and yet at the same time it manages to suggest the delicate, feminine features of a beautiful woman. With perfect coherence as a piece of sculpture, it demonstrates the symbolic representation of beauty and grace which is the ultimate aim of the Noh. It is believed this mask was once owned by the Kongo family of Noh actors and was carved by Tatsuemon, one of the "ten master carvers" of Noh's earliest days; if true, the fact that this carver of the masks of beautiful women could also create such a devilish woman is proof of great versatility.

34. Noh mask: Ko-omote. One often speaks of the "flower" of the Noh mask, meaning its essence, its spirit, and here in the young, pure, and noble features of the Ko-omote mask this "flower" is at its peak. The name, meaning "small mask," was probably chosen to indicate its artlessness and pleasantness. It is regarded as one of the supreme tests of the art of a carver of Noh masks, as the slightest vulgarity in the carver's conception of the pure young girl or in the execution will be revealed in the finished work. In the early days of the Noh only two kinds of female masks were needed—young and old—but as Noh became more complex many other types were required, such as those of a middle-aged woman who has tasted life's hardships and those of the purest of feminine beauty, of which this is an example. This mask is used in such plays as "Yuya," "Matsukaze," and "Izutsu."

35. Noh mask: Okina (Old Man). The Okina mask is used in a very special Noh play of the same name, sacred in character and quite unlike other Noh plays. The "play"—actually it is little but a dance—is believed to be much older than Noh. The mask is much more stylized than other Noh masks, the wrinkles forming a decorative pattern, and the hinged lower piece is more characteristic of Bugaku masks. The performance itself is reminiscent of the Gigaku, the stately dance of the old man being followed by a sprightly dance of a character called Sambaso, wearing a black mask in contrast with the white of the Okina mask. The similarity of this latter mask to the Taikofu mask of Gigaku *(Plate 1)* and Bugaku's Saisoro seems to bear out the supposition that Noh grew out of these earlier forms, and the stained and chipped condition of the remaining examples of early Okina masks bears witness to the great antiquity of this dance.

36. Noh mask: Uba (Old Woman). This is the typical Noh mask of an old woman, often being used in conjunction with the old-man mask called Jo. The two masks are similar in their drawn, stiff-muscled countenances, but the carver is always careful to express the difference of sex even in the sexlessness of old age. Himi Munetada, who is believed to have carved the mask shown here, is said to have been particularly good at rendering masks with an air of grief or distress. This mask well exemplifies the tragic qualities of Noh.

37. Noh mask: Yamauba (Witch). This too is an old-woman mask, that of a witch living far in the mountains. At the same time as it expresses old age, there is also a certain strength about it. The eyes are open wide, with shining metallic pupils, and fierce white teeth show through the large mouth, altogether producing a rough, wild effect.

38. Noh mask: Kagekiyo. Kagekiyo was a renowned warrior of the

Heike family in its losing struggles against the Genji family. Seeing all his efforts fail, he at last plucked out his eyes and fled into the mountains, where he was discovered many years later, a blind beggar and still discontent, by his daughter. The profound expression on this mask of the old Kagekiyo is one befitting the tragedy of a hero who could never achieve resignation. There are also two other types of Kagekiyo masks, suggesting that the carvers too were never quite content with their efforts to portray this complex character.

39. Noh mask: Sarutobide. *Tobide,* "jumping forth," refers to the type of mask with protruding eyes, and *saru,* "monkey," to the appearance of this particular mask. There are also masks called Otobide and Kotobide, meaning great and small jumping forth, referring to the degree by which the eyes protrude. All these Tobide masks are used by gods who, after first appearing on the stage in the meek masks of old men, next appear to demonstrate their divine power. Zeami, one of the founders of the Noh, says the masks were based upon the face of the statesman Sugawara Michizane (845–903) when he was angry, thereby suggesting that this mask predates the Noh. Unlike most Noh masks, the Tobide masks make no attempt to achieve a neutral expression but frankly express anger; this is possible because they are used only a short time during the latter part of a play.

40. Noh mask: Deija. The name of this mask means "golden serpent." It is similar to the Hannya mask *(Plate 33),* but is less feminine and more serpent-like. It is used only by the protagonist of "Dojoji" in the last scene. Its glittering, golden face adds greatly to its ghastliness. This is not carved from wood, but was built up from successive layers of lacquer and paper, the latter being paper amulets from Kumano and adding a mystic quality to the mask.

41. Kyogen mask: Oto. The name of this mask is an abbreviation of Otogozen, meaning "noble lady," and the mask is also frequently called by such pet names as Otafuku or Okame. Kyogen has no beautiful women but frequently uses the comic possibilities in a man's discovering that the girl he imagines to be a beauty is actually quite ugly. This mask is used in such comedies of disillusionment, and even though Oto is certainly far from beautiful, she nevertheless has a certain charming affability, contrasting with the cold charm of beautiful Noh ladies, which has made her a popular favorite.

42. Kyogen mask: Daikoku. Daikoku and Ebisu are the two gods of wealth and good luck, highly regarded of old and often still seen today. The perpetual and glorious smile on the full, round face is characteristic of this type of mask, making it most appropriate for the bright, light Kyogen. Kyogen masks often heighten their comic effect by being unexpectedly small when compared with the Noh masks.

43. KYOGEN MASK: KENTOKU. Both the name and the facial expression of this mask are mirth provoking. Kentoku was the name of a Buddhist priest who is said to have made such a face as this when he was suddenly exposed to a cold wind. We cannot be sure the name of this mask was derived from this incident, but certainly this is a grimace people often make when embarrassed. The fact that such a fleeting facial expression is here captured in frozen wood is in itself usually enough to set the audience to laughing. Oddly enough, in Kyogen this mask is used to represent the spirits of such diverse creatures as turtles, cows, dogs, crabs, or even sparrows. But then such unconventional illogic is one of the delightful attributes of Kyogen.

44. KYOGEN MASK: SARU (Monkey). Noh uses no animal masks, as they would be inappropriate for the tragic quality, but there are many such masks in Kyogen. Monkey masks are especially common, and are classified according to sex and age.

45. KYOGEN MASK: NOBORIHIGE. The name of this mask means "climbing whiskers." Note how the whiskers at the temples turn up instead of down, a comic touch which is reinforced by the missing teeth and the simplicity of the smiling face. This mask is used for the laughable spirits or ghosts of Kyogen.

46. KYOGEN MASK: KOBUAKU. This is a reduced-scale copy of the mask of a character called Buaku, one of the masterpieces of Kyogen masks. The mask expresses anger, while the crossed eyes take the sting out of the emotion and render it comic. It is a comical version of the angry mask of Beshimi in the Noh and is likewise used to represent demons, but what demon, however frightful, could retain his dignity when wearing such a mask?